WIDOWER'S HOUSES

AN UNPLEASANT PLAY

By

George BERNARD SHAW

NEW YORK
BRENTANO'S
1918

WIDOWERS' HOUSES

WIDOWERS' HOUSES

ACT I

In the garden restaurant of a hotel at Remagen on the Rhine, on a fine afternoon in August. Tables and chairs under the trees. The gate leading from the garden to the riverside is on the left. The hotel is on the right. It has a wooden annexe with an entrance marked Table d' Hôte. A waiter is in attendance.

A couple of English tourists come out of the hotel. The younger, Dr. Harry Trench, is about 24, stoutly built, thick in the neck, with close-cropped and black hair, with undignified medical student manners, frank, hasty, rather boyish. The other, Mr. William de Burgh Cokane, is older — probably over 40, possibly 50 — an ill-nourished, scanty-haired gentleman, with affected manners, fidgety, touchy, and constitutionally ridiculous in uncompassionate eyes.

COKANE (*on the threshold of the hotel, calling peremptorily to the waiter*). Two beers for us out here. (*The waiter goes for the beer. Cokane comes down into the garden.*) We have got the room with the best view in the hotel, Harry, thanks to my tact. We'll leave in the morning and do Mainz and Frankfurt. There is a very graceful female statue in the private house of a nobleman in Frankfurt— also a zoo. Next day, Nuremberg! finest collection of instruments of torture in the world.

TRENCH. All right. You look out the trains, will you? (*He takes out a Continental Bradshaw, and tosses it on one of the tables.*)

COKANE (*baulking himself in the act of sitting down*). Pah! the seat is all dusty. These foreigners are deplorably unclean in their habits.

TRENCH (*buoyantly*). Never mind: it don't matter, old chappie. Buck up, Billy, buck up. Enjoy yourself. (*He throws Cokane into the chair, and sits down opposite him, taking out his pipe, and singing noisily*)

> Pass about the Rhine wine: let it flow
> Like a free and flowing river——

COKANE (*scandalized*). In the name of common decency, Harry, will you remember that you are a gentleman and not a coster on Hampstead Heath on Bank Holiday? Would you dream of behaving like this in London?

TRENCH. Oh, rot! I've come abroad to enjoy myself: so would you if you'd just passed an examination after four years in the medical school and walking the hospital. (*Sings.*)

COKANE (*rising*). Trench: either you travel as a gentleman, or you travel alone. This is what makes Englishmen unpopular on the Continent. It may not matter before the natives; but the people who came on board the steamer at Coblentz are English. I have been uneasy all the afternoon about what they must think of us. Look at our appearance.

TRENCH. What is the matter with our appearance?

COKANE. Negligé, my dear fellow, negligé. On the steamboat a little negligé was quite en règle; but here, in this hotel, some of them are sure to dress for dinner; and you have nothing but that Norfolk jacket. How are they to know that you are well connected if you do not show it by your manners?

TRENCH. Pooh! the steamboat people were the scum

of the earth—Americans and all sorts. They may go hang themselves, Billy. I shall not bother about them. (*He strikes a match, and proceeds to light his pipe.*)

COKANE. Do drop calling me Billy in public, Trench. My name is Cokane. I am sure they were persons of consequence: you were struck with the distinguished appearance of the father yourself.

TRENCH (*sobered at once*). What! those people. (*He blows out the match and puts up his pipe.*)

COKANE (*following up his advantage triumphantly*). Here, Harry, here—at this hotel. I recognized the father's umbrella in the stand in the hall.

TRENCH (*with a touch of genuine shame*). I suppose I ought to have brought a change. But a lot of luggage is such a nuisance; and—(*rising abruptly*)—at all events we can go and have a wash. (*He turns to go into the hotel, but stops in consternation, seeing some people coming up to the riverside gate.*) Oh, I say. Here they are.

(*A lady and gentleman, followed by a porter with some light parcels, not luggage, but shop purchases, come into the garden. They are apparently father and daughter. The gentleman is 50, tall, well preserved and of upright carriage, with an incisive, domineering utterance and imposing style, which, with his strong aquiline nose and resolute clean-shaven mouth, give him an air of importance. He wears a light grey frock-coat with silk linings, a white hat, and a field-glass slung in a new leather case. A self-made man, formidable to servants, not easily accessible to any one. His daughter is a well-dressed, well-fed, good-looking, strong-minded young woman, presentably ladylike, but still her father's daughter. Nevertheless fresh and attractive, and none the worse for being vital and energetic rather than delicate and refined.*)

COKANE (*quickly taking the arm of Trench, who is staring as if transfixed*). Recollect yourself, Harry; presence of mind, presence of mind! (*He strolls with him towards the hotel. The waiter comes out with the beer.*) Kellner: cecilà est notre table. Est-ce-que vous comprenez Français?

WAITER. Yes, zare. All right, zare.

THE GENTLEMAN (*to his porter*). Place those things on that table. (*The porter does not understand.*)

WAITER (*interposing*). Zese zhentellmen are using zis table, zare. Would you mind——

THE GENTLEMAN (*severely*). You should have told me so before. (*To Cokane, with fierce condescension.*) I regret the mistake sir.

COKANE. Don't mention it, my dear sir; don't mention it. Retain the place, I beg.

TH3 GENTLEMAN (*coldly turning his back on him*). Thank you. (*To the porter.*) Place them on that table. (*The porter makes no movement until the gentleman points to the parcels and peremptorily raps the table.*)

PORTER. Ja wohl, gnädige Herr. (*He puts down the parcels.*)

THE GENTLEMAN (*taking out a handful of money*). Waiter.

WAITER (*awestruck.*) Yes, zare.

THE GENTLEMAN. Tea. For two. Out here.

WAITER. Yes, zare. (*He goes into the hotel.*)

(*The gentleman selects a small coin from his handful of money, and hands it to the porter, who receives it with a submissive touch to his cap, and goes out, not daring to speak. His daughter sits down and opens a parcel of photographs. The gentleman takes out a Baedeker; places a chair for himself; and then, instead of sitting down, looks truculently at Cokane, as if waiting for him to take himself off. Cokane, not at all abashed, resumes his place at the other table with an air of modest good breeding, and calls to Trench, who is prowling irresolutely in the background.*)

COKANE. Trench, my dear fellow, your beer is waiting for you. (*He drinks.*)

TRENCH (*glad of the excuse to come back to his chair*). Thank you, Cokane. (*He also drinks.*)

COKANE. By the way, Harry, I have often meant to ask you—is Lady Roxdale your mother's sister or your father's? (*This shot tells immediately. The gentleman is perceptibly interested.*)

TRENCH. My mother's, of course. What put that into your head?

COKANE. Nothing—I was just thinking—hm! She will expect you to marry, Harry: a doctor ought to marry.

TRENCH. What has she got to do with it?

COKANE. ' A great deal, dear boy. She looks forward to floating your wife in society in London.

TRENCH. What rot!

COKANE. Ah, you are young, dear boy: you are young. You don't know the importance of these things—apparently idle ceremonial trifles, really the springs and wheels of a great aristocratic system. (*The waiter comes back with the tea things, which he brings to the gentleman's table. Cokane rises and addresses the gentleman.*) My dear sir, excuse my addressing you; but I cannot help feeling that you prefer this table and that we are in your way.

THE GENTLEMAN (*graciously*). Thank you. Blanche, this gentleman very kindly offers us his table, if you would prefer it.

BLANCHE. Oh, thanks: it makes no difference.

THE GENTLEMAN (*to Cokane*). We are fellow travellers, I believe, sir.

COKANE. Fellow travellers and fellow countrymen. Ah, we rarely feel the charm of our own tongue until it reaches our ears under a foreign sky. You have no doubt noticed that?

THE GENTLEMAN (*a little puzzled*). Hm! From a romantic point of view, possibly, very possibly. As a matter of fact, the sound of English makes me feel at home; and I dislike feeling at home when I am abroad. It is not precisely what one goes to the expense for. (*He looks at Trench.*) I think this gentleman travelled with us also.

COKANE (*rising to act as master of the ceremonies. The gentleman and Trench rise also*). My valued friend, Dr. Trench. Trench, my dear fellow, allow me to introduce you to—er—? (*He looks enquiringly at the gentleman, waiting for the name.*)

THE GENTLEMAN. Permit me to shake your hand, Dr. Trench. My name is Sartorius; and I have the honour of being known to Lady Roxdale, who is, I believe, a near relative of yours. Blanche. (*She looks up.*) My friend Dr. Trench. (*They bow.*)

TRENCH. Perhaps I should introduce my friend Cokane to you, Mr. Sartorius—Mr. William de Burgh Cokane. (*Cokane makes an elaborate bow. Sartorius accepts it with dignity. The waiter meanwhile re-enters with teapot, hot water, etc.*)

SARTORIUS (*to the waiter*). Two more cups.

WAITER. Yes, zare. (*He goes back into the hotel.*)

BLANCHE. Do you take sugar, Mr. Cokane?

COKANE. Thank you. (*To Sartorius.*) This is really too kind. Harry: bring your chair around.

SARTORIUS. You are very welcome. (*Trench brings his chair to the tea table; and they all sit round it. The waiter returns with two more cups.*)

WAITER. Table d'hôte at 'alf past zix, zhentellmenn. Anyzing else now, zare?

SARTORIUS. No. You can go. (*The waiter goes.*)

COKANE (*very agreeably*). Do you contemplate a long stay here, Miss Sartorius?

BLANCHE. We were thinking of going on to Rolandseck. Is it as nice as this place?

COKANE. Harry: the Baedeker. Thank you. (*He consults the index, and looks out Rolandseck.*)

BLANCHE. Sugar, Dr. Trench?

TRENCH. Thanks. (*She hands him the cup, and looks meaningly at him for an instant. He looks down hastily, and glances apprehensively at Sartorius, who is preoccupied with a piece of bread and butter.*)

COKANE. Rolandseck appears to be an extremely interesting place. (*He reads.*) "It is one of the most beautiful and frequented spots on the river, and is surrounded with numerous villas and pleasant gardens, chiefly belonging to wealthy merchants from the Lower Rhine, and extending along the wooded slopes at the back of the village."

BLANCHE. That sounds civilized and comfortable. I vote we go there.

SARTORIUS. Quite like our place at Surbiton, my dear.

BLANCHE. Quite.

COKANE. You have a place down the river? Ah, I envy you.

SARTORIUS. No: I have merely taken a furnished villa at Surbiton for the summer. I live in Bedford Square. I am a vestryman and must reside in the parish.

BLANCHE. Another cup, Mr. Cokane?

COKANE. Thank you, no. (*To Sartorius.*) I presume you have been round this little place. Not much to see here, except the Appollinaris Church.

SARTORIUS (*scandalized*). The what!

COKANE. The Appollinaris Church.

SARTORIUS. A strange name to give a church. Very continental, I must say.

COKANE. Ah, yes, yes, yes. That is where our neighbours fall short sometimes, Mr. Sartorius: taste—taste is what they occasionally fail in. But in this instance they are not to blame. The water is called after the church, not the church after the water.

SARTORIUS (*as if this were an extenuating circumstance, but not a complete excuse*). I am glad to hear it. Is the church a celebrated one?

COKANE. Baedeker stars it.

SARTORIUS (*respectfully*). Oh, in that case I should like to see it.

COKANE (*reading*). "——erected in 1839 by Zwirner, the late eminent architect of the cathedral of Cologne, at the expense of Count Furstenburg-Stammheim."

SARTORIUS (*much impressed*). We must certainly see that, Mr. Cokane. I had no idea that the architect of Cologne cathedral lived so recently.

BLANCHE. Don't let us bother about any more churches, papa. They're all the same; and I'm tired to death of them.

SARTORIUS. Well, my dear, if you think it sensible to take a long and expensive journey to see what there is to be seen, and then go away without seeing it——

BLANCHE. Not this afternoon, papa, please.

SARTORIUS. My dear: I should like you to see everything. It is part of your education——

BLANCHE (*rising, with a petulant sigh*). Oh, my education. Very well, very well: I suppose I must go through with it. Are you coming, Dr. Trench? (*With a grimace.*) I'm sure the Johannis Church will be a treat for you.

COKANE (*laughing softly and archly*). Ah, excellent, excellent: very good, indeed. (*Seriously.*) But do you know, Miss Sartorius, there actually are Johannis churches here—several of them—as well as Appollinaris ones?

SARTORIUS (*sententiously taking out his field-glass and leading the way to the gate*). There is many a true word spoken in jest, Mr. Cokane.

COKANE (*accompanying him*). How true! How true! (*They go out together, ruminating profoundly. Blanche makes no movement to follow them. She watches them till they are safely out of sight, and then posts herself before Trench, look-*

ing at him with an enigmatic smile, which he returns with a half sheepish, half conceited grin.)

BLANCHE. Well! So you have done it at last.

TRENCH. Yes. At least Cokane's done it. I told you he'd manage it. He's rather an ass in some ways; but he has tremendous tact.

BLANCHE (*contemptuously*). Tact! That's not tact: that's inquisitiveness. Inquisitive people always have a lot of practice in getting into conversation with strangers. Why didn't you speak to my father yourself on the boat? You were ready enough to speak to me without any introduction.

TRENCH. I didn't particularly want to talk to him.

BLANCHE. It didn't occur to you, I suppose, that you put me in a false position by that.

TRENCH. Oh, I don't see that, exactly. Besides your father isn't an easy man to tackle. Of course, now that I know him, I see that he's pleasant enough; but then you've got to know him first, haven't you?

BLANCHE (*impatiently*). Everybody is afraid of papa— I'm sure I don't know why. (*She sits down again, pouting a little.*)

TRENCH (*tenderly*). However, it's all right now, isn't it? (*He sits near her.*)

BLANCHE (*sharply*). I don't know. How should I? You had no right to speak to me that day on board the steamer. You thought I was alone, because (*with false pathos*) I had no mother with me.

TRENCH (*protesting*). Oh, I say! Come! It was you who spoke to me. Of course I was only too glad of the chance; but on my word I shouldn't have moved an eyelid if you hadn't given me a lead.

BLANCHE. I only asked you the name of a castle. There was nothing unladylike in that.

TRENCH. Of course not. Why shouldn't you? (*With renewed tenderness.*) But it's all right now, isn't it?

BLANCHE (*softly—looking subtly at him*). Is it?

TRENCH (*suddenly becoming shy*). I—I suppose so. By the way, what about the Appollinaris Church? Your father expects us to follow him, doesn't he? (*He rises.*)

BLANCHE (*with suppressed resentment*). Don't let me detain you if you wish to see it.

TRENCH. Won't you come?

BLANCHE. No. (*She turns her face away moodily.*)

TRENCH (*alarmed*). I say: you're not offended, are you? (*She looks round at him for a moment with a reproachful film on her eyes.*) Blanche. (*She bristles instantly; overdoes it; and frightens him.*) I beg your pardon for calling you by your name; but I—er—— (*She corrects her mistake by softening her expression eloquently. He responds with a gush.*) You don't mind, do you? I felt sure you wouldn't somehow. Well, look here. I have no idea how you will receive this: it must seem horribly abrupt; but the circumstances do not admit of—the fact is, my utter want of tact —(*he flounders more and more, unable to see that she can hardly contain her eagerness.*) Now, if it were Cokane——

BLANCHE (*impatiently*). Cokane!

TRENCH (*terrified*). No, not Cokane. Though I assure you I was only going to say about him that——

BLANCHE. That he will be back presently with papa.

TRENCH (*stupidly*). Yes, they can't be very long now. I hope I am not detaining you.

BLANCHE. I thought you were detaining me because you had something to say.

TRENCH (*totally unnerved*). Not at all. At least nothing very particular. That is, I am afraid you would not think it very particular. Another time, perhaps——

BLANCHE. What other time? How do you know that we shall ever meet again? (*Desperately.*) Tell me now. I want you to tell me now.

TRENCH. Well, I was thinking that if we could make up

our minds to—or not to—at least—er—— (*He breaks down.*)

BLANCHE (*giving him up as hopeless*). I do not think there is much danger of y o u r making up your mind, Dr. Trench.

TRENCH (*stammering*). I only thought—— (*He stops and looks at her piteously. She hesitates a moment, and then puts her hands into his with calculated impulsiveness. He catches her in his arms with a cry of relief.*) Dear Blanche! I thought I should never have said it. I believe I should have stood stuttering here all day if you hadn't helped me out with it.

BLANCHE (*trying to get away from him*). I d i d n ' t help you out with it.

TRENCH (*holding her*). I don't mean that you did it on purpose, of course. Only instinctively.

BLANCHE (*still a little anxious*). But you haven't said anything.

TRENCH. What more can I say—than this? (*He kisses her again.*)

BLANCHE (*overcome by the kiss, but holding on to her point*). But Harry——

TRENCH (*delighted at the name*). Yes.

BLANCHE. When shall we be married?

TRENCH. At the first church we meet—the Appollinaris Church, if you like.

BLANCHE. No, but seriously. This is serious, Harry: you musn't joke about it.

TRENCH (*looking suddenly round to the riverside gate and quickly releasing her*). So! Here they are back again. (*She mutters something not unlike a suppressed oath. The waiter appears on the steps of the hotel, with a bell on which he gives a long ring. Cokane and Sartorius are seen returning by the river gate.*)

WAITER. Table d'hôte in dwendy minutes, ladies and zhentellmenn. (*He goes into the hotel.*)

SARTORIUS (*gravely*). I intended you to accompany us, Blanche.

BLANCHE. Yes, papa. We were just about to start.

SARTORIUS. We are rather dusty : we must make ourselves presentable at the table d'hôte. I think you had better come in with me, my child. Come. (*He offers Blanche his arm. The gravity of his manner overawes them all. Blanche silently takes his arm and goes into the hotel with him. Cokane, hardly less momentous than Sartorius himself, contemplates Trench with the severity of a judge.*)

COKANE (*with reprobation*). No, my dear boy. No, no. Never. I blush for you—was never so ashamed in my life. You have been taking advantage of that unprotected girl.

TRENCH (*hotly*). Cokane !

COKANE (*inexorable*). Her father seems to be a perfect gentleman. I obtained the privilege of his acquaintance ; I introduced you : I allowed him to believe that he might leave his daughter in your charge with absolute confidence. And what did I see on our return ?—what did her father see ? Oh, Trench, Trench ! No, my dear fellow, no, no. Bad taste, Harry, bad form !

TRENCH. Stuff ! There was nothing to see.

COKANE. Nothing to see ! She, a perfect lady, a person of the highest breeding, actually in your arms ; and you say there was nothing to see !—with a waiter there actually ringing a heavy bell to call attention to his presence. (*Lecturing him with redoubled severity.*) Have you no principles, Trench ? Have you no religious convictions ? Have you no acquaintance with the usages of society ? You actually kissed——

TRENCH. You didn't see me kiss her.

COKANE. We not only saw but h e a r d it : the report positively reverberated down the Rhine. Don't condescend to subterfuge, Trench.

TRENCH. Nonsense, my dear Billy. You——

COKANE. There you go again. Don't use that low abbreviation. How am I to preserve the respect of fellow travellers of position and wealth, if I am to be Billied at every turn? My name is William —William de Burgh Cokane.

TRENCH. Oh, bother! There, don't be offended, old chap. What's the use of putting your back up at every trifle? It comes natural to me to call you Bill: it suits you, somehow.

COKANE (*mortified*). You have no delicacy of feeling, Trench—no taste. I never mention it to any one; but nothing, I am afraid, will ever make a true gentleman of you. (*Sartorius appears on the threshold of the hotel.*) Here is my friend, Sartorius, coming, no doubt, to ask you for an explanation of your conduct. I really should not have been surprised to see him bring a horsewhip with him. I shall not intrude on the painful scene. (*Going.*)

TRENCH. Don't go, confound it. I don't want to meet him alone just now.

COKANE (*shaking his head*). Delicacy, Harry, delicacy. Good taste! Savoir faire! (*He walks away and disappears in the garden to the right. Trench tries to escape in the opposite direction by strolling off towards the garden entrance.*)

SARTORIUS (*mesmerically*). Dr. Trench.

TRENCH (*stopping and turning*). Oh, is that you, Mr. Sartorius? How did you find the church?

(*Sartorius, without a word, points to a seat. Trench, half hypnotized by his own nervousness and the impressiveness of Sartorius, sits down helplessly.*)

SARTORIUS (*also seating himself*). You have been speaking to my daughter, Dr. Trench?

TRENCH (*with an attempt at ease of manner*). Yes: we had a conversation—quite a chat, in fact—whilst you were at the church with Cokane. How did you get on with

Cokane, Mr. Sartorius? I always think he has such wonderful tact.

SARTORIUS (*ignoring the digression*). I have just had a word with my daughter, Dr. Trench; and I find her under the impression that something has passed between you which it is my duty as a father—the father of a motherless girl—to inquire into at once. My daughter, perhaps, foolishly, has taken you quite seriously ; and——

TRENCH. But——

SARTORIUS. One moment, if you will be so good. I have been a young man myself—younger, perhaps, than you would suppose from my present appearance. I mean, of course, in character. If you were not serious——

TRENCH (*ingeniously*). But I was perfectly serious. I want to marry your daughter, Mr. Sartorius. I hope you don't object.

SARTORIUS (*condescending to Trench's humility from the mere instinct to seize an advantage, and yet deferring to Lady Roxdale's relative*). So far, no. I may say that your proposal seems to be an honourable and straightforward one, and that is very gratifying to me personally.

TRENCH (*agreeably surprised*). Then I suppose we may consider the affair as settled. It's really very good of you.

SARTORIUS. Gently, Dr. Trench, gently. Such a transaction as this cannot be settled off-hand.

TRENCH. Not off-hand, no. There are settlements and things, of course. But it may be regarded as settled between ourselves, mayn't it ?

SARTORIUS. Hm ! Have you nothing further to mention ?

TRENCH. Only that—that—no: I don't know that I have, except that I love——

SARTORIUS (*interrupting*). Anything about your family, for example ? You do not anticipate any objection on their part, do you ?

TRENCH. Oh, they have nothing to do with it.

SARTORIUS (*warmly*). Excuse me, sir: they have a great deal to do with it. (*Trench is abashed.*) I am resolved that my daughter shall approach no circle in which she will not be received with the full consideration to which her education and her breeding (*here his self-control slips a little; and he repeats, as if Trench had contradicted him*)—I say, her breeding—entitle her.

TRENCH (*bewildered*). Of course not. But what makes you think my family won't like Blanche? Of course my father was a younger son; and I've had to take a profession and all that; so my people won't expect us to entertain them: they'll know we can't afford it. But they'll entertain us: they always ask me.

SARTORIUS. That won't do for me, sir. Families often think it due to themselves to turn their backs on newcomers whom they may not think quite good enough for them.

TRENCH. But I assure you my people aren't a bit snobbish. Blanche is a lady: that'll be good enough for them.

SARTORIUS (*moved*). I am glad you think so. (*Offers his hand. Trench, astonished, takes it.*) I think so myself. (*Sartorius presses Trench's hand gratefully and releases it.*) And now, Dr. Trench, since you have acted handsomely, you shall have no cause to complain of me. There shall be no difficulty about money: you shall entertain as much as you please: I will guarantee all that. But I must have a guarantee on my side that she will be received on equal terms by your family.

TRENCH. Guarantee!

SARTORIUS. Yes, a reasonable guarantee. I shall expect you to write to your relatives explaining your intention, and adding what you think proper as to my daughter's fitness for the best society. When you can show me a few letters from the principal members of your family, congratulating you in a fairly cordial way, I shall be satisfied. Can I say more?

TRENCH (*much puzzled, but grateful*). No indeed. You are really very good. Many thanks. Since you wish it, I'll write to my people. But I assure you you'll find them as jolly as possible over it. I'll make them write by return.

SARTORIUS. Thank you. In the meantime, I must ask you not to regard the matter as settled.

TRENCH. Oh! Not to regard the—I see. You mean between Blanche and——

SARTORIUS. I mean between you and Miss Sartorius. When I interrupted your conversation here some time ago, you and she were evidently regarding it as settled. In case difficulties arise, and the match—you see I call it a match—be broken off, I should not wish Blanche to think that she had allowed a gentleman to—to—(*Trench nods sympathetically*)—Quite so. May I depend on you to keep a fair distance, and so spare me the necessity of having to restrain an intercourse which promises to be very pleasant to us all ?

TRENCH. Certainly; since you prefer it. (*They shake hands on it.*)

SARTORIUS (*rising*). You will write to-day, I think you said ?

TRENCH (*eagerly*). I'll write now, before I leave here— straight off.

SARTORIUS. I will leave you to yourself then. (*He hesitates, the conversation having made him self-conscious and embarrassed; then recovers himself with an effort and adds with dignity, as he turns to go*) I am pleased to have come to an understanding with you. (*He goes into the hotel; and Cokane, who has been hanging about inquisitively, emerges from the shrubbery.*)

TRENCH. (*excitedly*). Billy, old chap, you're just in time to do me a favour. I want you to draft a letter for me to copy out.

COKANE. I came with you on this tour as a friend, Trench: not as a secretary.

TRENCH. Well, you'll write as a friend. It's to my Aunt Maria, about Blanche and me. To tell her, you know.

COKANE. Tell her about Blanche and you! Tell her about your conduct! Betray you, my friend; and forget that I am writing to a lady? Never!

TRENCH. Bosh, Billy: don't pretend you don't understand. We're engaged—engaged, my boy: what do you think of that? I must write by to-night's post. You are the man to tell me what to say. Come, old chap (*coaxing him to sit down at one of the tables*), here's a pencil. Have you a bit of—oh, here: this'll do: write it on the back of the map. (*He tears the map out of his Baedeker and spreads it face downwards on the table. Cokane takes the pencil and prepares to write.*) That's right. Thanks awfully, old chap! Now fire away. (*Anxiously.*) Be careful how you word it, though, Cokane.

COKANE (*putting down the pencil*). If you doubt my ability to express myself becomingly to Lady Roxdale——

TRENCH (*propitiating him*). All right, old fellow, all right: there's not a man alive who could do it half so well as you. I only wanted to explain. You see, Sartorius has got it into his head, somehow, that my people will snub Blanche; and he won't consent unless they send letters and invitations and congratulations and the deuce knows what not. So just put it in such a way that Aunt Maria will write by return saying she is delighted, and asking us—Blanche and me, you know—to stay with her, and so forth. You know what I mean. Just tell her all about it in a chatty way; and——

COKANE (*crushingly*). If you will tell me all about it in a chatty way, I daresay I can communicate it to Lady Roxdale with proper delicacy. What is Sartorius?

TRENCH (*taken aback*). I don't know: I didn't ask. It's a sort of question you can't very well put to a man—at least a man like him. Do you think you could word the letter so as to pass all that over? I really don't like to ask him.

COKANE. I can pass it over if you wish. Nothing easier. But if you think Lady Roxdale will pass it over, I differ from you. I may be wrong: no doubt I am. I generally am wrong, I believe; but that is my opinion.

TRENCH (*much perplexed*). Oh, confound it! What the deuce am I to do? Can't you say he's a gentleman: that won't commit us to anything. If you dwell on his being well off, and Blanche an only child, Aunt Maria will be satisfied.

COKANE. Henry Trench: when will you begin to get a little sense? This is a serious business. Act responsibly, Harry: act responsibly.

TRENCH. Bosh! Don't be moral!

COKANE. I am not moral, Trench. At least I am not a moralist: that is the expression I should have used—moral, but not a moralist. If you are going to get money with your wife, doesn't it concern your family to know how that money was made? Doesn't it concern you—you, Harry? (*Trench looks at him helplessly, twisting his fingers nervously. Cokane throws down the pencil and leans back with ostentatious indifference*). Of course it is no business of mine: I only throw out the suggestion. Sartorius may be a retired burglar for all I know. (*Sartorius and Blanche, ready for dinner, come from the hotel.*)

TRENCH. Sh! Here they come. Get the letter finished before dinner, like a good old chappie: I shall be awfully obliged to you.

COKANE (*impatiently*). Leave me, leave me: you disturb me. (*He waves him off and begins to write*).

TRENCH (*humbly and gratefully*). Yes, old chap. Thanks awfully.

(By this time Blanche has left her father and is strolling off toward the riverside. Sartorius comes down the garden, Baedeker in hand, and sits near Cokane, reading. Trench addresses him). You won't mind my taking Blanche in to dinner, I hope, sir?

SARTORIUS. By all means, Dr. Trench. Pray do so. *(He graciously waves him off to join Blanche. Trench hurries after her through the gate. The light reddens as the Rhenish sunset begins. Cokane, making wry faces in the agonies of composition, is disconcerted to find Sartorius' eye upon him.)*

SARTORIUS. I do not disturb you, I hope, Mr. Cokane.

COKANE. By no means. Our friend Trench has entrusted me with a difficult and delicate task. He has requested me, as a friend of the family, to write to them on a subject that concerns you.

SARTORIUS. Indeed, Mr. Cokane. Well, the communication could not be in better hands.

COKANE *(with an air of modesty)*. Ah, that is going too far, my dear sir, too far. Still, you see what Trench is. A capital fellow in his way, Mr. Sartorius, an excellent young fellow. But family communications like these require good manners. They require tact; and tact is Trench's weak point. He has an excellent heart, but no tact—none whatever. Everything depends on the way the matter is put to Lady Roxdale. But as to that, you may rely on me. I understand the sex.

SARTORIUS. Well, however she may receive it—and I care as little as any man, Mr. Cokane, how people may choose to receive me—I trust I may at least have the pleasure of seeing you sometimes at my house when we return to England.

COKANE *(overwhelmed)*. My d e a r sir! You express yourself in the true spirit of an English gentleman.

SARTORIUS. Not at all. You will always be most welcome. But I fear I have disturbed you in the composition of your letter. Pray resume it. I shall leave you to your-self. (*He pretends to rise, but checks himself to add*) Unless indeed I can assist you in any way ?—by clearing up any point on which you are not informed, for instance ; or even, if I may so far presume on my years, giving you the bene-fit of my experience as to the best way of wording the matter. (*Cokane looks a little surprised at this. Sartorius looks hard at him, and continues deliberately and meaningly*) I shall always be happy to help any friend of Dr. Trench's, in a n y way, to the best of my ability and of my means.

COKANE. My dear sir, you are really very good. Trench and I were putting our heads together over the letter just now ; and there certainly were one or two points on which we were a little in the dark. (*Scrupulously.*) But I would not permit Harry to question you. No. I pointed out to him that, as a matter of taste, it would be more delicate to wait until you volunteered the necessary information.

SARTORIUS. Hm ! May I ask what you have said, so far ?

COKANE. " My dear Aunt Maria." That is, Trench's dear Aunt Maria, my friend Lady Roxdale. You under-stand that I am only drafting a letter for Trench to copy.

SARTORIUS. Quite so. Will you proceed ; or would it help you if I were to suggest a word or two ?

COKANE (*effusively*). Your suggestions will be most valu-able, my dear sir, most welcome.

SARTORIUS. I think I should begin in some such way as this. " In traveling with my friend Mr. Cokane up the Rhine——"

COKANE (*murmuring as he writes*). Invaluable, invalu-able. The very thing. "—my friend Mr. Cokane up the Rhine——"

SARTORIUS. " I have made the acquaintance of"—or you may say "picked up" or "come across," if you think that would suit your friend's style better. We must not be too formal.

COKANE. "Picked up"! oh no: too dégagé, Mr. Sartorius, too dégagé. I should say, "had the privilege of becoming acquainted with."

SARTORIUS (*quickly*). By no means: Lady Roxdale must judge of that for herself. Let it stand as I said. "I have made the acquaintance of a young lady, the daughter of ———" (*He hesitates.*)

COKANE (*writing*). "acquaintance of a young lady, the daughter of"—yes?

SARTORIUS. "of" —you had better say "a gentleman."

COKANE (*surprised*). Of course.

SARTORIUS (*with sudden passion*). It is not of course, sir. (*Cokane, startled, looks at him with dawning suspicion. Sartorius recovers himself somewhat shamefacedly.*) Hm ! "—of a gentleman of considerable wealth and position———"

COKANE (*echoing him with a new note of coldness in his voice as he writes the last words*). "—and position."

SARTORIUS. "which, however, he has made entirely for himself." *Cokane, now fully enlightened, stares at him instead of writing.*) Have you written that?

COKANE (*expanding into an attitude of patronage and encouragement*). Ah, indeed. Quite so, quite so. (*He writes.*) "—entirely for himself." Just so. Proceed, Mr. Sartorius, proceed. Very clearly expressed.

SARTORIUS. "The young lady will inherit the bulk of her father's fortune, and will be liberally treated on her marriage. Her education has been of the most expensive and complete kind obtainable ; and her surroundings have been characterized by the strictest refinement. She is in every essential particular———"

COKANE (*interrupting*). Excuse the remark ; but don't you think this is rather too much in the style of a prospectus of the young lady ? I throw out the suggestion as a matter of taste.

SARTORIUS (*troubled*). Perhaps you are right. I am of course not dictating the exact words——

COKANE. Of course not : of course not.

SARTORIUS. But I desire that there may be no wrong impression as to my daughter's—er—breeding. As to myself——

COKANE. Oh, it will be sufficient to mention your profession, or pursuits, or—— (*He pauses ; and they look pretty hard at one another.*)

SARTORIUS (*very deliberately*). My income, sir, is derived from the rental of a very extensive real estate in London. Lady Roxdale is one of the head landlords ; and Dr. Trench holds a mortgage from which, if I mistake not, his entire income is derived. The truth is, Mr. Cokane, I am quite well acquainted with Dr. Trench's position and affairs ; and I have long desired to know him personally.

COKANE (*again obsequious, but still inquisitive*). What a remarkable coincidence! In what quarter is the estate situated, did you say ?

SARTORIUS. In London, sir. Its management occupies as much of my time as is not devoted to the ordinary pursuits of a gentleman. (*He rises and takes out his card case.*) The rest I leave to your discretion. (*He puts a card upon the table.*) That is my address at Surbiton. If it should unfortunately happen, Mr. Cokane, that this should end in a disappointment for Blanche, probably she would rather not see you afterwards. But if all turns out as we hope, Dr. Trench's best friends will then be our best friends.

COKANE (*rising and confronting Sartorius confidently, pencil and paper in hand*). Rely on me, Mr. Sartorius. The letter is already finished here (*points to his brain*). In five minutes it will be finished there (*points to the paper; nods to emphasize the assertion; and begins to pace up and down the garden, writing, and tapping his forehead from time to time as he goes, with every appearance of severe intellectual exertion.*)

SARTORIUS (*calling through the gate after a glance at his watch.*) Blanche.

BLANCHE (*replying in the distance*). Yes.

SARTORIUS. Time, my dear. (*He goes in to the table d'hôte.*)

BLANCHE (*nearer*). Coming. (*She comes back through the gate, followed by Trench.*)

TRENCH (*in a half whisper, as Blanche goes towards the table d'hôte*). Blanche : stop—one moment. (*She stops.*) We must be careful when your father is by. I had to promise him not to regard anything as settled until I hear from my people at home.

BLANCHE (*chilled*). Oh, I see. Your family may object to me ; and then it will be all over between us. They are almost sure to.

TRENCH (*anxiously*). Don't say that, Blanche ; it sounds as if you didn't care. I hope you regard it as settled. You haven't made any promise, you know.

BLANCHE (*earnestly*). Yes, I have : I promised papa too. But I have broken my promise for your sake. I suppose I am not so conscientious as you. And if the matter is not to be regarded as settled, family or no family, promise or no promise, let us break it off here and now.

TRENCH (*intoxicated with affection*). Blanche : on my most sacred honour, family or no family, promise or no promise—— (*The waiter reappears at the table d'hôte entrance, ringing his bell loudly.*) Damn that noise!

COKANE (*as he comes to them, flourishing the letter*). Finished, dear boy, finished. Done to a turn, punctually to the second. C'est fini, mon cher garçon, c'est fini. (*Sartorius returns.*)

SARTORIUS. Will you take Blanche in, Dr. Trench? (*Trench takes Blanche in to the table d'hôte.*)   Is the letter finished, Mr. Cokane?

COKANE (*with an author's pride, handing his draft to Sartorius*).   There!   (*Sartorius takes it, and reads it, nodding gravely over it with complete approval.*)

SARTORIUS (*returning the draft*).   Thank you, Mr. Cokane. You have the pen of a ready writer.

COKANE (*as they go in together*).   Not at all, not at all.   A little tact, Mr. Sartorius, a little knowledge of the world, a little experience of women——(*The act drop descends and cuts off the rest of the speech.*)

END OF ACT I.

ACT II

in the library of a handsomely appointed villa at Surbiton on a sunny forenoon in September. Sartorius is busy at a writing table, littered with business letters, on the left. He sits facing the window, which is in the right wall. The fireplace, decorated for summer, is behind him. Between the table and the window Blanche, in her prettiest frock, sits reading " The Queen." The door, painted, like all the woodwork, in the blackest shade of red, with brass fittings, and moulded posts and pediment, is in the middle of the back wall. All the walls are lined with smartly tooled books, fitting into their places like bricks. A library ladder stands in the corner.

SARTORIUS. Blanche.

BLANCHE. Yes, papa.

SARTORIUS. I have some news here.

BLANCHE. What is it?

SARTORIUS. I mean news for you—from Trench,

BLANCHE (*with affected indifference*). Indeed?

SARTORIUS. "Indeed?"! Is that all you have to say to me? Oh, very well. (*He resumes his work. Silence.*)

BLANCHE. What do his people say, papa?

SARTORIUS. His people, I don't know. (*Still busy. Another pause.*)

BLANCHE. What does he say?

SARTORIUS. He! He says nothing. (*He folds a letter leisurely and looks for the envelope.*) He prefers to communicate the result of his—where did I put that?—oh, here. Yes, he prefers to communicate the result in person.

BLANCHE (*springing up*). Oh, papa! When is he coming?

SARTORIUS. If he walks from the station, he may arrive in the course of the next half-hour. If he drives, he may be here any moment.

BLANCHE (*making hastily for the door*). Oh!

SARTORIUS. Blanche.

BLANCHE. Yes, papa.

SARTORIUS. You will of course not meet him until he has spoken to me.

BLANCHE (*hypocritically*). Of course not, papa. I shouldn't have thought of such a thing.

SARTORIUS. That is all. (*She is going, when he puts out his hand, and says with fatherly emotion.*) My dear child. (*She responds by going over to kiss him. A tap at the door.*) Come in. (*Lickcheese enters, carrying a black hand-bag. He is a shabby, needy man, with dirty face and linen, scrubby beard and whiskers, going bald. A nervous, wiry, pertinacious sort of human terrier judged by his mouth and eyes, but miserably apprehensive and servile before Sartorius. He bids Blanche "Good morning, miss"; and she passes out with a slight and contemptuous recognition of him.*)

LICKCHEESE. Good morning, sir.

SARTORIUS (*harsh and peremptory*). Good morning.

LICKCHEESE (*taking a little sack of money from his bag*). Not much this morning, sir. I have just had the honour of making Dr. Trench's acquaintance, sir.

SARTORIUS (*looking up from his writing, displeased*). Indeed?

LICKCHEESE. Yes, sir. Dr. Trench asked his way of me, and was kind enough to drive me from the station.

SARTORIUS. Where is he, then?

LICKCHEESE. I left him in the hall, with his friend, sir. I should think he is speaking to Miss Sartorius.

SARTORIUS. Hm!   What do you mean by his friend?

LICKCHEESE. There is a Mr. Cokane with him, sir.

SARTORIUS. I see you have been talking to him, eh?

LICKCHEESE. As we drove along: yes, sir.

SARTORIUS (*sharply*). Why did you not come by the nine o'clock train?

LICKCHEESE. I thought——

SARTORIUS. It cannot be helped now; so never mind what you thought.   But do not put off my business again to the last moment.   Has there been any further trouble about the St. Giles' property?

LICKCHEESE. The Sanitary Inspector has been complaining again about number 13 Robbins's Row.   He says he'll bring it before the vestry.

SARTORIUS. Did you tell him that I am on the vestry?

LICKCHEESE. Yes, sir.

SARTORIUS. What did he say to that?

LICKCHEESE. Said he supposed so, or you wouldn't dare to break the law so scand'lous.   I only tell you what he said.

SARTORIUS. Hm!   Do you know his name!

LICKCHEESE. Yes, sir.   Speakman.

SARTORIUS. Write it down in the diary for the day of the next vestry meeting.   I will teach Mr. Speakman his duty —his duty to members of the vestry.

LICKCHEESE (*doubtfully*). The vestry can't dismiss him, sir.   He's under the Local Government Board.

SARTORIUS. I did not ask you that.   Let me see the books.   (*Lickcheese produces the rent book, and hands it to Sartorius; then makes the desired entry in the diary on the table, watching Sartorius with misgiving as the rent book is examined.   Sartorius frowns and rises.*) £1: 4s. for repairs to No. 13.   What does this mean?

LICKCHEESE. Well, sir, it was the staircase on the third floor.   It was downright dangerous: there weren't but three whole steps in it, and no handrail. I thought it best to have a few boards put in.

SARTORIUS. Boards! Firewood, sir, firewood! They will burn every stick of it. You have spent twenty-four shillings of my money on firewood for them.

LICKCHEESE. There ought to be stone stairs, sir: it would be a saving in the long run. The clergyman says——

SARTORIUS. What! who says?

LICKCHEESE. The clergyman, sir, only the clergyman. Not that I make much account of him; but if you knew how he has worried me over that staircase——

SARTORIUS. I am an Englishman; and I will suffer no clergyman to interfere in my business. (*He turns suddenly on Lickcheese.*) Now look here, Mr. Lickcheese! This is the third time this year that you have brought me a bill of over a pound for repairs. I have warned you repeatedly against dealing with these tenement houses as if they were mansions in a West-end square. I have had occasion to warn you too against discussing my affairs with strangers. You have chosen to disregard my wishes. You are discharged.

LICKCHEESE (*dismayed*). Oh, sir, don't say that.

SARTORIUS (*fiercely*). You are discharged.

LICKCHEESE. Well, Mr. Sartorius, it is hard, so it is. No man alive could have screwed more out of them poor destitute devils for you than I have, or spent less in doing it. I have dirtied my hands at it until they're not fit for clean work hardly ; and now you turn me——

SARTORIUS (*interrupting him menacingly*). What do you mean by dirtying your hands? If I find that you have stepped an inch outside the letter of the law, Mr. Lickcheese, I will prosecute you myself. The way to keep your hands clean is to gain the confidence of your employers. You will do well to bear that in mind in your next situation.

THE PARLOUR MAID (*opening the door*). Mr. Trench and

Mr. Cokane. (*Cokane and Trench come in, Trench festively dressed and in the highest spirits, Cokane highly self-satisfied.*)

SARTORIUS. How do you do, Dr. Trench? Good morning Mr. Cokane. I am pleased to see you here. Mr. Lickcheese, you will place your accounts and money on the table : I will examine them and settle with you presently. (*Lickcheese retires to the table, and begins to arrange his accounts, greatly depressed.*)

TRENCH (*glancing at Lickcheese*). I hope we're not in the way.

SARTORIUS. By no means. Sit down, pray. I fear you have been kept waiting.

TRENCH (*taking Blanche's chair*). Not at all. We've only just come in. (*He takes out a packet of letters and begins untying them.*)

COKANE (*going to a chair nearer the window, but stopping to look admiringly round before sitting down*). You must be happy here with all these books, Mr. Sartorius. A literary atmosphere.

SARTORIUS (*resuming his seat*). I have not looked into them. They are pleasant for Blanche occasionally when she wishes to read. I chose the house because it is on gravel. The death rate is very low.

TRENCH (*triumphantly*). I have any amount of letters for you. All my people are delighted that I am going to settle. Aunt Maria wants Blanche to be married from her house. (*He hands Sartorius a letter.*)

SARTORIUS. Aunt Maria !

COKANE. Lady Roxdale, my dear sir : he means Lady Roxdale. Do express yourself with a little more tact, my dear fellow.

TRENCH. Lady Roxdale, of course. Uncle Harry——

COKANE. Sir Harry Trench. His godfather, my dear sir, his godfather.

TRENCH. Just so. The pleasantest fellow for his age you

ever met.   He offers us his house at St. Andrews for a couple of months, if we care to pass our honeymoon there. (*Handing Sartorius another letter.*)   It's the sort of house nobody can live in, you know ; but it's a nice thing for him to offer.   Don't you think so?

SARTORIUS (*preoccupied with the letters*). No doubt. These seem very gratifying, Dr. Trench.

TRENCH. Yes; aren't they? Aunt Maria has really behaved like a brick.   If you read the postscript you'll see she spotted Cokane's hand in my letter. (*Chuckling.*)   He wrote it for me.

SARTORIUS (*glancing at Cokane*). Indeed?   Mr. Cokane evidently did it with great tact.

COKANE (*returning the glance*).   Don't mention it.

TRENCH (*buoyantly*).   Well, what do you say now, Mr. Sartorius?   May we regard the matter as settled at last!

SARTORIUS. Quite settled. (*He rises and offers his hand. Trench, glowing with gratitude, rises and shakes it vehemently, unable to find words for his feelings.*)

COKANE (*coming between them*). Allow me to congratulate you both.   (*Shakes hands with the two at the same time.*)

SARTORIUS. And now, gentlemen, I have a word to say to my daughter.   Dr. Trench, you will not, I hope, grudge me the pleasure of breaking this news to her: I have had to disappoint her more than once since I last saw you.   Will you excuse me for ten minutes?

COKANE (*in a flush of friendly protest*). My dear sir, can you ask?

TRENCH. Certainly.

SARTORIUS. Thank you.   (*He goes out.*)

TRENCH (*still chuckling*). He won't have any news to break, poor old boy: she's seen all the letters already.

COKANE. I must say your behaviour has been far from straightforward, Harry.   You have been carrying on a clandestine correspondence.

LICKCHEESE (*stealthily*). Gentlemen———

TRENCH }
COKANE } (*turning—they had forgotten his presence*). Hallo!

LICKCHEESE (*coming between them very humbly, but in mortal anxiety and haste*). Look here, gentlemen. (*To Trench.*) You, sir, I address myself to more partic'lar. Will you say a word in my favour to the guv'nor? He's just given me the sack; and I have four children looking to me for their bread. A word from you, sir, on this happy day, might get him to take me on again.

TRENCH (*embarrassed*). Well, you see, Mr. Lickcheese, I don't see how I can interfere. I'm very sorry, of course.

COKANE. Certainly you cannot interfere. It would be in the most execrable taste.

LICKCHEESE. Oh, gentlemen, you are young; and you don't know what loss of employment means to the like of me. What harm would it do you to help a poor man? Just listen to the circumstances, sir. I only———

TRENCH (*moved but snatching at an excuse for taking a high tone in avoiding the unpleasantness of helping him*). No: I had rather not. Excuse my saying plainly that I think Mr. Sartorius is not a man to act hastily or harshly. I have always found him very fair and generous; and I believe he is a better judge of the circumstances than I am.

COKANE (*inquisitive*). I think you ought to hear the circumstances, Harry. It can do no harm. Hear the circumstances by all means.

LICKCHEESE. Never mind, sir: it ain't any use. When I hear that man called generous and fair!—well, never mind.

TRENCH (*severely*). If you wish me to do anything for you, Mr. Lickcheese, let me tell you that you are not going the right way about it in speaking ill of Mr. Sartorius.

LICKCHEESE. Have I said one word against him, sir? I leave it to your friend: have I said a word?

COKANE. True, true. Quite true. Harry: be just.

LICKCHEESE. Mark my words, gentlemen: he'll find what a man he's lost the very first week's rents the new man'll bring him. You'll find the difference yourself, Dr. Trench, if you or your children come into the property. I have got money when no other collector alive would have wrung it out. And this is the thanks I get for it! Why, see here, gentlemen! Look at that bag of money on the table. Hardly a penny of that but there was a hungry child crying for the bread it would have bought. But I got it for him—screwed and worried and bullied it out of them. I—look here, gentlemen: I'm pretty well seasoned to the work; but there's money there that I couldn't have taken if it hadn't been for the thought of my own children depending on me for giving him satisfaction. And because I charged him four-and-twenty shillin' to mend a staircase that three women have been hurt on, and that would have got him prosecuted for manslaughter if it had been let go much longer, he gives me the sack. Wouldn't listen to a word, though I would have offered to make up the money out of my own pocket—aye, and am willing to do it still if you will only put in a word for me, sir.

TRENCH (*aghast*). You took money that ought to have fed starving children! Serve you right! If I had been the father of one of those children, I'd have given you something worse than the sack. I wouldn't say a word to save your soul, if you have such a thing. Mr. Sartorius was quite right.

LICKCHEESE (*staring at him, surprised into contemptuous amusement in the midst of his anxiety*). Just listen to this! Well, you a r e an innocent young gentleman. Do you suppose he sacked me because I was too hard? Not a bit of it: it was because I wasn't hard enough. I never heard him say he was satisfied yet—no, nor he wouldn't, not if

I skinned 'em alive.   I don't say he's the worst landlord in London : he couldn't be worse than some ; but he's no better than the worst I ever had to do with.   And, though I say it, I'm better than the best collector he ever done business with.   I have screwed more and spent less on his properties than any one would believe that knows what such properties are.   I know my merits, Dr. Trench, and will speak for myself if no one else will.

TRENCH. What sort of properties ?   Houses ?

LICKCHEESE. Tenement houses, let from week to week by the room or half-room—aye, or quarter-room.   It pays when you know how to work it, sir.   Nothing like it.   It's been calculated on the cubic foot of space, sir, that you can get higher rents letting by the room than you can for a mansion in Park Lane.

TRENCH. I hope Mr. Sartorius hasn't much of that sort of property, however it may pay.

LICKCHEESE. He has nothing else, sir ; and he shows his sense in it too.   Every few hundred pounds he could scrape together he bought old houses with—houses that you wouldn't hardly look at without holding your nose.   He has 'em in St. Giles's : he has 'em in Marylebone : he has 'em in Bethnal Green.   Just look how he lives himself, and you'll see the good of it to him.   He likes a low death-rate and a gravel soil for himself, he does.   You come down with me to Robbins's Row ; and I'll show you a soil and a death-rate, so I will !   And, mind you, it's me that makes it pay him so well.   Catch him going down to collect his own rents !   Not likely !

TRENCH. Do you mean to say that all his property—all his means—come from this sort of thing ?

LICKCHEESE. Every penny of it, sir. (*Trench, overwhelmed, has to sit down.*)

COKANE (*looking compassionately at him*). Ah, my dear fellow, the love of money is the root of all evil.

LICKCHEESE. Yes, sir; and we'd all like to have the tree growing in our garden.

COKANE (*revolted*). Mr. Lickcheese, I did not address myself to you. I do not wish to be severe with you; but there is something peculiarly repugnant to my feelings in the calling of a rent collector.

LICKCHEESE. It's no worse than many another. I have my children looking to me.

COKANE. True: I admit it. So has our friend Sartorius. His affection for his daughter is a redeeming point—a redeeming point, certainly.

LICKCHEESE. She's a lucky daughter, sir. Many another daughter has been turned out upon the streets to gratify his affection for her. That's what business is, sir, you see. Come sir, I think your friend will say a word for me now he knows I'm not in fault.

TRENCH (*rising angrily*). I will not. It's a damnable business from beginning to end; and you deserve no better luck for helping in it. I've seen it all among the out-patients at the hospital; and it used to make my blood boil to think that such things couldn't be prevented.

LICKCHEESE (*his suppressed spleen breaking out*). Oh indeed, sir. But I suppose you will take your share when you marry Miss Blanche, all the same. (*Furiously.*) Which of us is the worse, I should like to know—me that wrings the money out to keep a home over my children, or you that spend it and try to shove the blame on to me?

COKANE. A most improper observation to address to a gentleman, Mr. Lickcheese. A most revolutionary sentiment.

LICKCHEESE. Perhaps so. But then, Robbins's Row ain't a school for manners. You collect a week or two there—you're welcome to my place if I can't keep it for myself—and you'll hear a little plain speaking, so you will.

COKANE (*with dignity*). Do you know to whom you are speaking, my good man?

LICKCHEESE (*recklessly*). I know well enough who I'm speaking to. What do I care for you, or a thousand such! I'm poor; that's enough to make a rascal of me. No consideration for me—nothing to be got by saying a word for me! (*Suddenly cringing to Trench.*) Just a word, sir. It would cost you nothing. (*Sartorius appears at the door unobserved.*) Have some feeling for the poor.

- TRENCH. I'm afraid you have shown very little, by your own confession.

LICKCHEESE (*breaking out again*). More than your precious father-in-law, anyhow. I—— (*Sartorius's voice, striking in with deadly calmness, paralyzes him.*)

SARTORIUS. You will come here to-morrow not later than ten, Mr. Lickcheese, to conclude our business. I shall trouble you no further to-day. (*Lickcheese, cowed, goes out amid dead silence. Sartorius continues, after an awkward pause.*) He is one of my agents, or rather was ; for I have unfortunately had to dismiss him for repeatedly disregarding my instructions. (*Trench says nothing. Sartorius throws off his embarrassment, and assumes a jocose, rallying air, unbecoming to him under any circumstances, and just now almost unbearably jarring.*) Blanche will be down presently, Harry (*Trench recoils*)—I suppose I must call you Harry now. What do you say to a stroll through the garden, Mr. Cokane? We are celebrated here for our flowers.

COKANE. Charmed, my dear sir, charmed. Life here is an idyll—a perfect idyll. We were just dwelling on it.

SARTORIUS (*slyly*). Harry can follow with Blanche. She will be down directly.

TRENCH (*hastily*). No. I can't face her just now.

SARTORIUS (*rallying him*). Indeed! Ha, ha! (*The laugh, the first they have heard from him, sets Trench's teeth on edge. Cokane is taken aback, but instantly recovers himself.*)

COKANE. Ha! ha! ha! Ho! ho!——

TRENCH. But you don't understand.

SARTORIUS. Oh, I think we do, I think we do. Eh,
Mr. Cokane? Ha! ha!

COKANE. I should think we do. Ha! ha! ha!

(*They go out together, laughing at him. He collapses into
a chair, shuddering in every nerve. Blanche appears at the
door. Her face lights up when she sees that he is alone. She
trips noiselessly to the back of his chair and clasps her hands
over his eyes. With a convulsive start and exclamation he
springs up and breaks away from her.*)

BLANCHE (*astonished*). Harry!

TRENCH (*with distracted politeness*). I beg your pardon, I
was thinking—won't you sit down.

BLANCHE (*looking suspiciously at him*). Is anything the
matter? (*She sits down slowly near the writing table. He
takes Cokane's chair.*)

TRENCH. No. Oh no.

BLANCHE. Papa has not been disagreeable, I hope.

TRENCH No : I have hardly spoken to him since I was
with you. (*He rises; takes up his chair; and plants it be-
side hers. This pleases her better. She looks at him with
her most winning smile. A sort of sob breaks from him; and
he catches her hands and kisses them passionately. Then,
looking into her eyes with intense earnestness, he says*) Blanche:
are you fond of money ?

BLANCHE (*gaily*). Very. Are you going to give me any ?

TRENCH (*wincing*). Don't make a joke of it : I'm serious.
Do you know that we shall be very poor ?

BLANCHE. Is that what made you look as if you had neu-
ralgia ?

TRENCH (*pleadingly*). My dear : it's no laughing matter.
Do you know that I have a bare seven hundred a year to
live on ?

BLANCHE. How dreadful !

TRENCH. Blanche : it's very serious indeed : I assure you it is.

BLANCHE. It would keep me rather short in my house-keeping, dearest boy, if I had nothing of my own. But papa has promised me that I shall be richer than ever when we are married.

TRENCH. We must do the best we can with seven hundred. I think we ought to be self-supporting.

BLANCHE. That's just what I mean to be, Harry. If I were to eat up half your £700, I should be making you twice as poor; but I am going to make you twice as rich instead. (*He shakes his head.*) Has papa made any difficulty ?

TRENCH (*rising with a sigh and taking his chair back to its former place*). No, none at all. (*He sits down dejectedly. When Blanche speaks again her face and voice betray the beginning of a struggle with her temper.*)

BLANCHE. Harry, are you too proud to take money from my father !

TRENCH. Yes, Blanche : I am too proud.

BLANCHE (*after a pause*). That is not nice to me, Harry.

TRENCH. You must bear with me Blanche. I—I can't explain. After all, it's very natural.

BLANCHE. Has it occurred to you that I may be proud, too ?

TRENCH. Oh, that's nonsense. No one will accuse y o u of marrying for money.

BLANCHE. No one would think the worse of me if I did, or of you either. (*She rises and begins to walk restlessly about.*) We really cannot live on seven hundred a year, Harry ; and I don't think it quite fair of you to ask me merely because you are afraid of people talking.

TRENCH. It is not that alone, Blanche.

BLANCHE. What else is it, then ?

TRENCH. Nothing. I——

BLANCHE (*getting behind him, and speaking with forced playfulness as she bends over him, her hands on his shoulders*). Of course it's nothing.   Now don't be absurd, Harry : be good ; and listen to me : I know how to settle it.   You are too proud to owe anything to me ; and I am too proud to owe anything to you.   You have seven hundred a year. Well, I will take just seven hundred a year from papa at first ; and then we shall be quits.   Now, now, Harry, you know you have not a word to say against that.

TRENCH. It's impossible.

BLANCHE. Impossible !

TRENCH. Yes, impossible.   I have resolved not to take any money from your father.

BLANCHE. But he will give the money to me : not to you.

TRENCH. It's the same thing.   (*With an effort to be sentimental.*)   I love you too well to see any distinction.   (*He puts up his hand half-heartedly: she takes it over his shoulder with equal indecision.   They are both trying hard to conciliate one another.*)

BLANCHE. That's a very nice way of putting it, Harry ; but I am sure there is something I ought to know.   Has papa been disagreeable ?

TRENCH. No : he has been very kind—to me, at least. It's not that.   It's nothing you can guess, Blanche.   It would only pain you—perhaps offend you.   I don't mean, of course, that we shall live always on seven hundred a year. I intend to go at my profession in earnest, and work my fingers to the bone.

BLANCHE (*playing with his fingers, still over his shoulder*). But I shouldn't like you with your fingers worked to the bone, Harry.   I must be told what the matter is.   (*He takes his hand quickly away; she flushes angrily; and her voice is no longer even an imitation of the voice of a lady as she exclaims.*)   I hate secrets ; and I don't like to be treated as if I were a child.

TRENCH (*annoyed by her tone*). There's nothing to tell. I don't choose to trespass on your father's generosity : that's all.

BLANCHE. You had no objection half an hour ago, when you met me in the hall, and showed me all the letters. Your family doesn't object. Do y o u object ?

TRENCH (*earnestly*). I do not indeed. It's only a question of money.

BLANCHE (*imploringly, the voice softening and refining for the last time*). Harry : there's no use in our fencing in this way. Papa will never consent to my being absolutely dependent on you ; and I don't like the idea of it myself. If you even mention such a thing to him you will break off the match : you will indeed.

TRENCH (*obstinately*). I can't help that.

BLANCHE (*white with rage*). You can't help——! Oh, I'm beginning to understand. I will save you the trouble. You can tell papa that *I* have broken off the match ; and then there will be no further difficulty.

TRENCH (*taken aback*). What do you mean, Blanche ? Are you offended ?

BLANCHE. Offended ! How dare you ask me ?

TRENCH. Dare !

BLANCHE. How much more manly it would have been to confess that you were trifling with me that time on the Rhine ! Why did you come here to-day ? Why did you write to your people ?

TRENCH. Well, Blanche, if you are going to lose your temper——

BLANCHE. That's no answer. You depended on your family to get you out of your engagement ; and they did not object : they were only too glad to be rid of you. You were not mean enough to stay away, and not manly enough to tell the truth. You thought you could provoke me to break the engagement : that is so like a man—to try and put

the woman in the wrong. Well, you have your way: I
release you. I wish you had opened my eyes by downright
brutality—by striking me—by anything rather than shuffling
as you have done.

TRENCH (*hotly*). Shuffle ! If I had thought you capable
of turning on me like this, I should never have spoken to
you. I have a good mind never to speak to you again.

BLANCHE. You shall not—not ever. I will take care of
that. (*Going to the door.*)

TRENCH (*alarmed.*) What are you going to do ?

BLANCHE. To get your letters—your false letters, and your
presents—your hateful presents, to return them to you. I
am very glad it is all broken off ; and if—(*as she puts her
hand to the door it is opened from without by Sartorius, who
enters and shuts it behind him.*)

SARTORIUS (*interrupting her severely*). Hush, pray,
Blanche : you are forgetting yourself : you can be heard all
over the house. What is the matter ?

BLANCHE (*too angry to care whether she is overheard or
not*). You had better ask h i m. He has some excuse about
money.

SARTORIUS. Excuse ! Excuse for what ?

BLANCHE. For throwing me over.

TRENCH (*vehemently*). I declare I never——

BLANCHE (*interrupting him still more vehemently*). You
did. You did. You are doing nothing else—— (*Trench
begins repeating his contradiction and she her assertion; so
that they both speak angrily together.*)

SARTORIUS (*in desperation at the noise*). Silence. (*Still
more formidably.*) Silence. (*They obey. He proceeds
firmly.*) Blanche, you must control your temper: I will
not have these repeated scenes within hearing of the servants. Dr. Trench will answer for himself to me. You
had better leave us. •(*He opens the door, and calls*) Mr.
Cokane, will you kindly join us here.

COKANE *(in the conservatory)*. Coming, my dear sir, coming. *(He appears at the door.)*

BLANCHE. I am sure I have no wish to stay. I hope I shall find you alone when I come back. *(An inarticulate exclamation bursts from Trench. She goes out, passing Cokane resentfully. He looks after her in surprise; then looks questioningly at the two men. Sartorius shuts the door with an angry stroke, and turns to Trench.)*

SARTORIUS *(aggressively)*. Sir——

TRENCH *(interrupting him more aggressively)*. Well, sir !

COKANE *(getting between them)*. Gently, dear boy, gently. Suavity, Harry, suavity.

SARTORIUS *(mastering himself)*. If you have anything to say to me, Dr. Trench, I will listen to you patiently. You will then allow me to say what I have to say on my part.

TRENCH *(ashamed)*. I beg your pardon. Of course, yes. Fire away.

SARTORIUS. May I take it that you have refused to fulfil your engagement with my daughter?

TRENCH. Certainly not: your daughter has refused to fulfil her engagement with me. But the match is broken off, if that is what you mean.

SARTORIUS. Dr. Trench: I will be plain with you. I know that Blanche has a strong temper. It is part of her strong character and her physical courage, which is greater than that of most men, I can assure you. You must be prepared for that. If this quarrel is only Blanche's temper you may take my word for it that it will be over before to-morrow. But I understood from what she said just now that you have made some difficulty on the score of money.

TRENCH *(with renewed excitement)*. It was Miss Sartorius who made that difficulty. I shouldn't have minded that so much, if it hadn't been for the things she said. She showed that she doesn't care t h a t (*snapping his fingers*) for me.

COKANE (*soothingly*). Dear boy——

TRENCH. Hold your tongue, Billy: it's enough to make a man wish he'd never seen a woman. Look here, Mr. Sartorius: I put the matter to her as delicately and considerately as possible, never mentioning a word of my reasons, but just asking her to be content to live on my own little income; and yet she turned on me as if I had behaved like a savage.

SARTORIUS. Live on your income! Impossible: my daughter is accustomed to a proper establishment. Did I not expressly undertake to provide for that? Did she not tell you I promised her to do so?

TRENCH. Yes, I know all about that, Mr. Sartorius; and I'm greatly obliged to you; but I'd rather not take anything from you except Blanche herself.

SARTORIUS. And why did you not say so before?

TRENCH. No matter why. Let us drop the subject.

SARTORIUS. No matter! But it d o e s matter, sir. I insist on an answer. Why did you not say so before?

TRENCH. I didn't know before.

SARTORIUS (*provoked*). Then you ought to have known your own mind before entering into such a very serious engagement. (*He flings angrily away across the room and back.*)

TRENCH (*much injured*). I o u g h t to have known. Cokane: is this reasonable? (*Cokane's features are contorted by an air of judicial consideration; but he says nothing; and Trench, again addressing Sartorius, but with a marked diminution of respect, continues*) How the deuce could I have known? You didn't tell me.

SARTORIUS. You are trifling with me, sir. You say that you did not know your own mind before.

TRENCH. I say nothing of the sort. I say that I did not know where your money came from before.

SARTORIUS. That is not true, sir. I——

COKANE. Gently, my dear sir. Gently, Harry, dear boy. Suaviter in modo: fort——

TRENCH. Let him begin, then. What does he mean by attacking me in this fashion?

SARTORIUS. Mr. Cokane: you will bear me out. I was explicit on the point. I said I was a self-made man; and I am not ashamed of it.

TRENCH. You are nothing of the sort. I found out this morning from your man—Lickcheese, or whatever his confounded name is—that your fortune has been made out of a parcel of unfortunate creatures that have hardly enough to keep body and soul together—made by screwing, and bullying, and driving, and all sorts of pettifogging tyranny.

SARTORIUS (*outraged*). Sir! (*They confront one another threateningly.*)

COKANE (*softly*). Rent must be paid, dear boy. It is inevitable, Harry, inevitable. (*Trench turns away petulantly. Sartorius looks after him reflectively for a moment; then resumes his former deliberate and dignified manner, and addresses Trench with studied consideration, but with a perceptible condescension to his youth and folly.*)

SARTORIUS. I am afraid, Dr. Trench, that you are a very young hand at business; and I am sorry I forgot that for a moment or so. May I ask you to suspend your judgment until we have a little quiet discussion of this sentimental notion of yours?—if you will excuse me for calling it so. (*He takes a chair, and motions Trench to another on his right.*)

COKANE. Very nicely put, my dear sir. Come, Harry, sit down and listen; and consider the matter calmly and judicially. Don't be headstrong.

TRENCH. I have no objection to sit down and listen; but I don't see how that can make black white; and I am tired of being turned on as if I were in the wrong. (*He sits down. Cokane sits at his elbow, on his right. They compose themselves for a conference.*)

SARTORIUS. I assume, to begin with, Dr. Trench, that you are not a Socialist, or anything of that sort.

TRENCH. Certainly not. I am a Conservative—at least, if I ever took the trouble to vote, I should vote for the Conservative and against the other fellow.

COKANE. True blue, Harry, true blue!

SARTORIUS. I am glad to find that so far we are in perfect sympathy. I am, of course, a Conservative; not a narrow or prejudiced one, I hope, nor at all opposed to true progress, but still a sound Conservative. As to Lickcheese, I need say no more about him than that I have dismissed him from my service this morning for a breach of trust; and you will hardly accept his testimony as friendly or disinterested. As to my business, it is simply to provide homes suited to the small means of very poor people, who require roofs to shelter them just like other people. Do you suppose I can keep up these roofs for nothing!

TRENCH. Yes: that is all very fine; but the point is, what sort of homes do you give them for their money? People must live somewhere, or else go to jail. Advantage is taken of that to make them pay for houses that are not fit for dogs. Why don't you build proper dwellings, and give fair value for the money you take?

SARTORIUS (*pitying his innocence*). My young friend, these poor people do not know how to live in proper dwellings: they would wreck them in a week. You doubt me: try it for yourself. You are welcome to replace all the missing banisters, handrails, cistern lids and dusthole tops at your own expense; and you will find them missing again in less than three days—burnt, sir, every stick of them. I do not blame the poor creatures: they need fires, and often have no other way of getting them. But I really cannot spend pound after pound in repairs for them to pull down, when I can barely get them to pay me four and sixpence a week for a room, which is the recognized fair London rent. No, gentlemen : when people are very poor, you c a n n o t help them, no matter how much you may sympathize with them. It does them more harm than good in the long run. I prefer to save my money in order to provide additional houses for the homeless, and to lay by a little for Blanche. (*He looks at them. They are silent : Trench unconvinced, but talked down ; Cokane humanely perplexed. Sartorius bends his brows ; comes forward in his chair as if gathering himself together for a spring ; and addresses himself, with impressive significance, to Trench.*) And now, Dr. Trench, may I ask what y o u r income is derived from !

TRENCH (*defiantly*). From interest—not from houses. My hands are clean as far as that goes. Interest on a mortgage.

SARTORIUS (*forcibly*). Yes : a mortgage on m y property. When I, to use your own words, screw, and bully, and drive these people to pay what they have freely undertaken to pay me, I cannot touch one penny of the money they give me until I have first paid you your £700 out of it. What Lickcheese did for me, I do for you. He and I are alike intermediaries : y o u are the principal. It is because of the risks I run through the poverty of my tenants that you exact interest from me at the monstrous and exorbitant rate of seven per cent, forcing me to exact the uttermost farthing in my turn from the tenants. And yet, Dr. Trench, you have not hesitated to speak contemptuously of me because I have applied my industry and forethought to the management of o u r property, and am maintaining it by the same honourable means.

COKANE (*greatly relieved*). Admirable, my dear sir, excellent ! I felt instinctively that Trench was talking unpractical nonsense. Let us drop the subject, my dear boy :

you only make an ass of yourself when you meddle in business matters. I told you it was inevitable.

TRENCH (*dazed*). Do you mean to·say that I am just as bad as you are ?

COKANE. Shame, Harry, shame ! Grossly bad taste ! Be a gentleman. Apologize.

SARTORIUS. Allow me, Mr. Cokane. (*To Trench.*) If, when you say you are just as bad as I am, you mean that you are just as powerless to alter the state of society, then you are unfortunately quite right. (*Trench does not at once reply. He stares at Sartorius, and then hangs his head and gazes stupidly at the floor, morally beggared, with his clasped knuckles between his knees, a living picture of disillusion. Cokane comes sympathetically to him and puts an encouraging hand on his shoulder.*)

COKANE (*gently*). Come, Harry, come ! Pull yourself together. You owe a word to Mr. Sartorius.

TRENCH (*still stupefied, slowly unlaces his fingers; puts his hands on his knees, and lifts himself upright ; pulls his waistcoat straight with a tug ; and turns to Sartorius with an attempt to take his disenchantment philosophically*). Well, people who live in glass houses have no right to throw stones. But, on my honour, I never knew that my house was a glass one until you pointed it out. I beg your pardon. (*He offers his hand .*)

SARTORIUS. Say no more, Harry : your feelings do you credit : I assure you I feel exactly as you do, myself. Every man who has a heart must wish that a better state of things was practicable.   But unhappily it is not.

TRENCH (*a little consoled*). I suppose not.

COKANE. Not a doubt of it, my dear sir ; not a doubt of it.   The increase of the population is at the bottom of it all.

SARTORIUS (*to Trench*). I trust I have convinced you that you need no more object to Blanche sharing my fortune, than I need object to her sharing yours.

TRENCH (*with dull wistfulness*). It seems so. We're all in the same swim, it appears. I hope you will excuse my making such a fuss.

SARTORIUS. Not another word. In fact, I thank you for refraining from explaining the nature of your scruples to Blanche : I admire that in you, Harry. Perhaps it will be as well to leave her in ignorance.

TRENCH (*anxiously*). But I must explain now. You saw how angry she was.

SARTORIUS. You had better leave that to me. (*He looks at his watch, and rings the bell.*) Lunch is nearly due : while you are getting ready for it I can see Blanche ; and I hope the result will be quite satisfactory to us all. (*The parlour maid answers the bell; he addresses her with his habitual peremptoriness.*) Tell Miss Blanche I want her.

THE PARLOUR MAID (*her face falling expressively*). Yes, sir. (*She turns reluctantly to go.*)

SARTORIUS (*on second thoughts*). Stop. (*She stops.*) My love to Miss Blanche : and I am alone here and would like to see her for a moment if she is not busy.

THE PARLOUR MAID (*relieved*). Yes sir. (*She goes out.*)

SARTORIUS. I will show you your room, Harry. I hope you will soon be perfectly at home in it. You also, Mr. Cokane, must learn your way about here. Let us go before Blanche comes. (*He leads the way to the door.*)

COKANE (*cheerily, following him*). Our little discussion has given me quite an appetite.

TRENCH (*moodily*). It has taken mine away. (*They go out, Sartorius holding the door for them. He is following when the parlour maid reappears. She is a snivelling, sympathetic creature, and is on the verge of tears.*)

SARTORIUS. Well, is Miss Blanche coming ?

THE PARLOUR MAID. Yes sir. I think so sir.

SARTORIUS. Wait here until she comes ; and tell her that I will be back in a moment.

THE PARLOUR MAID. Yes, sir. (*She comes into the room. Sartorius looks suspiciously at her as she passes him. He half closes the door and follows her.*)

SARTORIUS (*lowering his voice*). What is the matter with you?

THE PARLOUR MAID (*whimpering*). Nothing, sir.

SARTORIUS (*at the same pitch, more menacingly*). Take care how you behave yourself when there are visitors present. Do you hear?

THE PARLOUR MAID. Yes, sir. (*Sartorius goes out.*)

SARTORIUS (*outside*). Excuse me: I had a word to say to the servant. (*Trench is heard replying, "Not at all," Cokane "Don't mention it, my dear sir." The murmur of their voices passes out of hearing. The parlour maid sniffs; dries her eyes; goes to one of the bookcases; and takes some brown paper and a ball of string from a drawer. She puts them on the table and wrestles with another sob. Blanche comes in, with a jewel box in her hands. Her expression is that of a strong and determined woman in an intense passion. The maid looks at her with a mixture of abject wounded affection and bodily terror.*)

BLANCHE (*looking around*). Where's my father?

THE PARLOUR MAID (*tremulously propitiatory*). He left word he'd be back directly, miss. I'm sure he won't be long. Here's the paper and string all ready, miss. (*She spreads the paper on the table.*) Can I do the parcel for you, miss?

BLANCHE. No. Mind your own business. (*She empties the box on the sheet of brown paper. It contains a packet of letters, a ring, and a set of gold bangles. At sight of them she has a paroxysm of passion, which she relieves by dashing the box to the floor. The maid submissively picks it up and puts it on the table, again sniffing and drying her eyes.*) What are you crying for?

THE PARLOUR MAID (*plaintively*). You speak so brutal to

me, Miss Blanche; and I do love you so. I'm sure no one else would stay and put up with what I have to put up with.

BLANCHE. Then go. I don't want you. Do you hear. Go.

THE PARLOUR MAID (*piteously, falling on her knees*). Oh no, Miss Blanche. Don't send me away from you: don't——

BLANCHE (*with fierce disgust*). Agh! I hate the sight of you. (*The maid, wounded to the heart, cries bitterly.*) Hold your tongue. Are those two gentlemen gone?

THE PARLOUR MAID (*weeping*). Oh, how could you say such a thing to me, Miss Blanche—me that——

BLANCHE (*seizing her by the hair and throat*). Stop that noise, I tell you, unless you want me to kill you.

THE PARLOUR MAID (*protesting and imploring, but in a carefully subdued voice*). Let me go, Miss Blanche: you know you'll be sorry: you always are. Remember how dreadfully my head was cut last time.

BLANCHE (*raging*). Answer me, will you? Have they gone?

THE PARLOUR MAID. Lickcheese has gone, looking dreadf—— (*she breaks off with a stifled cry as Blanche's fingers tighten furiously on her.*)

BLANCHE. Did I ask you about Lickcheese? You beast: you know who I mean: you're doing it on purpose.

THE PARLOUR MAID (*in a gasp*). They're staying to lunch.

BLANCHE (*looking intently into her face*). He ?——

THE PARLOUR MAID (*whispering with a sympathetic nod*). Yes, miss. (*Blanche slowly releases her and stands upright with clenched fists and set face. The parlour maid, recogniz- ing the passing of the crisis of passion and fearing no further violence, sits discomfitedly on her heels, and tries to arrange her hair and cap, whimpering a little with exhaustion and soreness.*) Now you've set my hands all trembling; and I shall jingle the things on the tray at lunch so that everybody will notice me. It's too bad of you, Miss Bl—— (*Sartorius coughs outside.*)

BLANCHE (*quickly*). Sh! Get up. (*The parlour maid hastily gets up, and goes out as demurely as she can, passing Sartorius on her way to the door. He glances sternly at her and comes to Blanche. The parlour maid shuts the door softly behind her.*)

SARTORIUS (*mournfully*). My dear: can you not make a little better fight with your temper?

BLANCHE (*panting with the subsidence of her fit*). No I can't. I won't. I do my best. Nobody who really cares for me gives me up because of my temper. I never show my temper to any of the servants but that girl; and she is the only one that will stay with us.

SARTORIUS. But, my dear, remember that we have to meet our visitors at luncheon presently. I have run down before them to say that I have arranged that little difficulty with Trench. It was only a piece of mischief made by Lickcheese. Trench is a young fool; but it is all right now.

BLANCHE. I don't want to marry a fool.

SARTORIUS. Then you will have to take a husband over thirty, Blanche. You must not expect too much, my child. You will be richer than your husband, and, I think, cleverer too. I am better pleased that it should be so.

BLANCHE (*seizing his arm*). Papa.

SARTORIUS. Yes, my dear.

BLANCHE. May I do as I like about this marriage; or must I do as you like?

SARTORIUS (*uneasily*). Blanche——

BLANCHE. No, papa; you m u s t answer me.

SARTORIUS (*abandoning his self-control, and giving way recklessly to his affection for her*). You shall do as you like now and always, my beloved child. I only wish to do as my own darling pleases.

BLANCHE. Then I will not marry him. He has played fast and loose with me. He thinks us beneath him, he is ashamed of us; he dared to object to being benefited by you—as if it were not natural for him to owe you everything; and yet the money tempted him after all. (*Suddenly throwing her arms hysterically about his neck.*) Papa, I don't want to marry: I only want to stay with you and be happy as we have always been. I hate the thought of being married: I don't care for him: I don't want to leave you. (*Trench and Cokane return; but she can hear nothing but her own voice and does not notice them.*) Only send him away: promise me that you will send him away and keep me here with you as we have always—(*seeing Trench.*) Oh! (*She hides her face on her father's breast.*)

TRENCH (*nervously*). I hope we are not intruding.

SARTORIUS (*formidably*). Dr. Trench : my daughter has changed her mind.

TRENCH (*disconcerted*). Am I to understand——

COKANE (*striking in in his most vinegary manner*). I think, Harry, under the circumstances, we have no alternative but to seek luncheon elsewhere.

TRENCH. But, Mr. Sartorius, have you explained——?

SARTORIUS (*straight in Trench's face*). I have explained, sir. Good morning. (*Trench, outraged, advances a step. Blanche sinks away from her father into a chair. Sartorius stands his ground rigidly.*)

TRENCH (*turning away indignantly*). Come on, Cokane.

COKANE. Certainly, Harry, certainly. (*Trench goes out, very angry. The parlour maid, with a tray jingling in her hands, passes outside.*) You have disappointed me, sir, very acutely. Good morning. (*He follows Trench.*)

END OF ACT II.

ACT III

*The drawing-room in Sartorius's house in Bedford Square.
Winter evening: fire burning, curtains drawn and lamps
lighted. Sartorius and Blanche are sitting glumly near the
fire. The Parlour Maid, who has just brought in coffee, is
placing it on a small table between them. There is a large
table in the middle of the room. The pianoforte, a grand, is
on the left, with a photographic portrait of Blanche on a
miniature easel on the top. Two doors, one on the right
further forward than the fireplace, leading to the study; the
other at the back, on the left, leading to the lobby. Blanche
has her work basket at hand, and is knitting. Sartorius,
closer to the fire, has a newspaper. The Parlour Maid goes
out.*

SARTORIUS. Blanche, my love.

BLANCHE. Yes.

SARTORIUS. I had a long talk to the doctor to-day about our
going abroad.

BLANCHE (*impatiently*). I am quite well; and I will not go
abroad. I loathe the very thought of the Continent. Why
will you bother me so about my health?

SARTORIUS. It was not about your health, Blanche, but
about my own.

BLANCHE (*rising*). Yours! (*She goes anxiously to him.*)
Oh, papa, there is nothing the matter with you, I hope?

SARTORIUS. There will be — there must be, Blanche, long
before you begin to consider yourself an old woman.

BLANCHE. But there is nothing the matter now?

SARTORIUS. Well, my dear, the doctor says I need change, travel, excitement——

BLANCHE. Excitement!   You need excitement!   (*She laughs joylessly, and sits down on the rug at his feet.*)   How is it, papa, that you, who are so clever with everybody else, are not a bit clever with me?   Do you think I can't see through your little plan to take me abroad?   Since I will not be the invalid and allow you to be the nurse, you are to be the invalid and I am to be the nurse.

SARTORIUS. Well, Blanche, if you will have it that you are well and have nothing preying on your spirits, I must insist on being ill and have something preying on mine. And indeed, my girl, there is no use in our going on as we have for the last four months.   You have not been happy; and I have been far from comfortable.   (*Blanche's face clouds: she turns away from him and sits dumb and brooding. He waits in vain for some reply; then adds in a lower tone*) Need you be so inflexible, Blanche?

BLANCHE (*pained and rigid*).   I thought you admired inflexibility: you have always prided yourself on it.

SARTORIUS. Nonsense, my dear, nonsense.   I have had to give in often enough.   And I could show you plenty of soft fellows who have done as well as I, and enjoyed themselves more, perhaps.   If it is only for the sake of inflexibility that you are standing out——

BLANCHE. I am not standing out.   I don't know what you mean.   (*She tries to rise and go away.*)

SARTORIUS (*catching her arm and arresting her on her knees*). Come, my child: you must not trifle with me as if I were a stranger.   You are fretting because——

BLANCHE (*violently twisting herself free and speaking as she rises*).   If you say it, papa, I will kill myself.   It is not true. If he were here on his knees to-night, I would walk out of the house sooner than endure it.   (*She goes out excitedly.*

Sartorius, greatly troubled, turns again to the fire with a heavy sigh.)

SARTORIUS (*gazing gloomily into the glow*). Now if I fight it out with her, no more comfort for months! I might as well live with my clerk or my servant. And if I give in now, I shall have to give in always. Well, I can't help it. I have stuck to having my own way all my life; but there must be an end to that drudgery some day. She is young: let her have her turn at it. (*The parlour maid comes in.*)

THE PARLOUR MAID. Please sir, Mr. Lickcheese wants to see you very particular. On important business—y o u r business, he told me to say.

SARTORIUS. Mr. Lickcheese! Do you mean Lickcheese who used to come here on my business?

THE PARLOUR MAID. Yes, sir. But indeed, sir, you'd scarcely know him.

SARTORIUS (*frowning*). Hm! Starving, I suppose. Come to beg?

THE PARLOUR MAID (*intensely repudiating the idea*). O-o-o-o-h NO, sir. Quite the gentleman, sir! Sealskin overcoat, sir! Come in a hansom, all shaved and clean! I'm sure he's come into a fortune, sir.

SARTORIUS. Hm! Show him up.

(*Lickcheese, who has been waiting at the door, instantly comes in. The change in his appearance is dazzling. He is in evening dress, with an overcoat lined throughout with furs presenting all the hues of the tiger. His shirt is fastened at the breast with a single diamond stud. His silk hat is of the glossiest black; a handsome gold watch chain hangs like a garland on his filled out waistcoat; he has shaved his whiskers and grown a moustache, the ends of which are waxed and pointed. As Sartorius stares speechless at him, he stands, smiling, to be admired, intensely enjoying the effect he is producing. The parlour maid, hardly less pleased with her own share in this coup-de-théâtre, goes out beaming, full of the news for the kitchen. Lickcheese clinches the situation by a triumphant nod at Sartorius.*)

SARTORIUS (*bracing himself—hostile*). Well?

LICKCHEESE. Quite well, Sartorius, thankee.

SARTORIUS. I was not asking after your health, sir, as you know, I think, as well as I do. What is your business?

LICKCHEESE. Business that I can take elsewhere if I meet with less civility than I please to put up with, Sartorius. You and me is man and man now. It was money that used to be my master, and not you, don't think it. Now that I'm independent in respect of money——

SARTORIUS (*crossing determinedly to the door, and holding it open*). You can take your independence out of my house, then. I won't have it here.

LICKCHEESE (*indulgently*). Come, Sartorius, don't be stiffnecked. I come here as a friend to put money in your pocket. No use in your lettin' on to me that you're above money. Eh?

SARTORIUS (*hesitates, and at last shuts the door, saying guardedly*). How much money?

LICKCHEESE (*victorious, going to Blanche's chair and beginning to take off his overcoat*). Ah! there you speak like yourself, Sartorius. Now suppose you ask me to sit down and make myself comfortable.

SARTORIUS (*coming from the door*). I have a mind to put you downstairs by the back of your neck, you infernal blackguard.

LICKCHEESE (*not a bit ruffled, takes off his overcoat and hangs it on the back of Blanche's chair, pulling a cigar case out of one of his pockets as he does so*). You and me is too much of a pair for me to take anything you say in bad part, Sartorius. 'Ave a cigar.

SARTORIUS. No smoking here: this is my daughter's room. However, sit down, sit down. (*They sit.*)

LICKCHEESE. I' bin gittin' orn a little since I saw you last.

SARTORIUS. So I see.

LICKCHEESE. I owe it partly to you, you know. Does that surprise you?

SARTORIUS. It doesn't concern me.

LICKCHEESE. So you think, Sartorius, because it never did concern you how *I* got on, so long as I got y o u on by bringing in the rents. But I picked up something for myself down at Robbins's Row.

SARTORIUS. I always thought so. Have you come to make restitution?

LICKCHEESE. You wouldn't take it if I offered it to you, Sartorius. It wasn't money: it was knowledge — knowledge of the great public question of the Housing of the Working Classes. You know there's a Royal Commission on it, don't you?

SARTORIUS. Oh, I see. You've been giving evidence.

LICKCHEESE. Giving evidence! Not me. What good would that do me! Only my expenses; and that not on the professional scale, neither. No: I gev no evidence. But I'll tell you what I did. I kep' it back, just to oblige one or two people whose feelings would have been hurt by seeing their names in a bluebook as keeping a fever den. Their Agent got so friendly with me over it that he put his name on a bill of mine to the tune of— well, no matter: it gave me a start; and a start was all I ever wanted to get on my feet. I've got a copy of the first report of the Commission in the pocket of my overcoat. (*He rises and gets at his overcoat, from a pocket of which he takes a bluebook.*) I turned down the page to show you: I thought you'd like to see it. (*He doubles the book back at the place indicated, and hands it to Sartorius.*)

SARTORIUS. So blackmail is the game, eh? (*He puts the book on the table without looking at it, and strikes it emphatically with his fist.*) I don't care t h a t for my name being in bluebooks. My friends don't read them; and I'm neither a Cabinet Minister nor a candidate for Parliament. There's nothing to be got out of me on that lay.

LICKCHEESE (*shocked*). Blackmail! Oh, Mr. Sartorius, do you think I would let out a word about your premises? Round on an old pal! no: that ain't Lickcheese's way. Besides, they know all about you already. Them stairs that you and me quarrelled about, they was a whole afternoon examining the clergyman that made such a fuss—you remember?—about the women that was hurt on it. He made the worst he could of it, in an ungentlemanly, unchristian spirit. I wouldn't have that clergyman's disposition for worlds. Oh no: that's not what was in my thoughts.

SARTORIUS. Come, come, man: what w a s in your thoughts? Out with it.

LICKCHEESE (*with provoking deliberation, smiling and looking mysteriously at him*). You ain't spent a few hundreds in repairs since we parted, have you? (*Movement of impatience from Sartorius: Lickcheese goes on soothingly.*) Now don't fly out at me. I know a landlord that owned as beastly a slum as you could find in London, down there by the Tower. By my advice that man put half the houses into first-class repair, and let the other half to a new Company—the North Thames Iced Mutton Depot Company, of which I held a few shares—promoters' shares. And what was the end of it, do you think?

SARTORIUS. Smash! I suppose.

LICKCHEESE. Smash! not a bit of it. Compensation, Mr. Sartorius, compensation. Do you understand that?

SARTORIUS. Compensation for what?

LICKCHEESE. Why, the land was wanted for an extension of the Mint; and the Company had to be bought out, and the buildings compensated for. Somebody has to know these things beforehand, you know, no matter how dark they're kept.

SARTORIUS (*interested, but cautious*). Well?

LICKCHEESE. Is that all you have to say to me, Mr. Sartorius? "Well"! as if I was next door's dog! Suppose I'd got wind of a new street that would knock down Robbins's Row and turn Burke's Walk into a frontage worth thirty pounds a foot!—would you say no more to me than (*mimicking*) "Well"? (*Sartorius hesitates, looking at him in great doubt: Lickcheese rises and exhibits himself.*) Come, look at my get-up, Mr. Sartorius. Look at this watchchain! Look at the corporation I've got on me! Do you think all that came from keeping my mouth shut? No, it came from keeping my ears and eyes open. (*Blanche comes in, followed by the parlour maid, who has a silver tray on which she collects the coffee cups. Sartorius, impatient at the interruption, rises and motions Lickcheese to the door of the study.*)

SARTORIUS. Sh. We must talk this over in the study. There is a good fire there, and you can smoke. Blanche: an old friend of ours.

LICKCHEESE. And a kind one to me. I hope I see you well, Miss Blanche.

BLANCHE. Why it's Mr. Lickcheese! I hardly knew you.

LICKCHEESE. I find you a little changed yourself, miss.

BLANCHE (*hastily*). Oh, I am the same as ever. How are Mrs. Lickcheese and the chil——

SARTORIUS (*impatiently*). We have business to transact, Blanche. You can talk to Mr. Lickcheese afterwards. Come on. (*Sartorius and Lickcheese go into the study. Blanche, surprised at her father's abruptness, looks after them for a moment. Then, seeing Lickcheese's overcoat on her chair, she takes it up, amused, and looks at the fur.*)

THE PARLOUR MAID. Oh, we are fine, ain't we, Miss Blanche? I think Mr. Lickcheese must have come into a legacy. (*Confidentially.*) I wonder what he can want with the master, Miss Blanche!   He brought him this big book.   (*She shows the bluebook to Blanche.*)

BLANCHE (*her curiosity roused—taking the book*). Let me see.   (*She looks at it.*)   There's something about papa in it.   (*She sits down and begins to read.*)

THE PARLOUR MAID (*folding the tea-table and putting it out of the way*). He looks ever so much younger, Miss Blanche, don't he.   I couldn't help laughing when I saw him with his whiskers shaved off: it do look so silly when you're not accustomed to it.   (*No answer from Blanche.*) You haven't finished your coffee, miss: I suppose I may take it away.   (*No answer.*)   Oh, you a r e interested in Mr. Lickcheese's book, miss.   (*Blanche springs up.   The parlour maid looks at her face, and instantly hurries out of the room on tiptoe with her tray.*)

BLANCHE. So that was why he would not touch the money.   (*She tries to tear the book across; but that is impossible; and she throws it violently into the fireplace.   It falls into the fender.*)   Oh, if only a girl could have no father, no family, just as I have no mother !   Clergyman!—beast! "The worst slum landlord in London."   "Slum landlord."   Oh!   (*She covers her face with her hands and sinks shuddering into the chair on which the overcoat lies.   The study door opens.*)

LICKCHEESE (*in the study*). You just wait five minutes. I'll fetch him.   (*Blanche snatches a piece of work from her basket and sits erect and quiet, stitching at it.   Lickcheese comes back, speaking to Sartorius, who follows him.*)   He lodges round the corner in Gower Street; and my private 'ansom's at the door.   By your leave, Miss Blanche (*pulling gently at his overcoat.*)

BLANCHE (*rising*). I beg your pardon. I hope I haven't crushed it.

LICKCHEESE (*with the coat on*). You're welcome to crush it again n o w, Miss Blanche.   Don't say good evening to me, miss: I'm coming back, presently—me and a friend or two. Ta, ta, Sartorius: I shan't be long. (*He goes out. Sartorius looks about for the bluebook.*)

BLANCHE. I thought we were done with Lickcheese.

SARTORIUS. Not quite yet, I think. He left a book here for me to look over—a large book in a blue paper cover. Has the girl put it away? (*He sees it in the fender; looks at Blanche; and adds.*) Have you seen it!

BLANCHE. No. Yes. (*Angrily.*) No, I have not seen it. What have I to do with it! (*Sartorius picks the book up and dusts it; then sits down quietly to read. After a glance up and down the columns, he nods assentingly, as if he found there exactly what he expected.*)

SARTORIUS. It's a curious thing, Blanche, that the Parliamentary gentlemen who write such books as these, should be so ignorant of practical business. One would suppose, to read this, that we are the most grasping, grinding, heartless pair in the world, you and I.

BLANCHE. Is it not true—about the state of the houses, I mean?

SARTORIUS (*calmly*). Oh, quite true.

BLANCHE. Then is it not our fault?

SARTORIUS. My dear, if we made the houses any better, the rents would have to be raised so much that the poor people would be unable to pay, and would be thrown homeless on the streets.

BLANCHE. Well, turn them out and get in a respectable class of people. Why should we have the disgrace of harbouring such wretches?

SARTORIUS (*opening his eyes*). That sounds a little hard on them, doesn't it, my child?

BLANCHE. Oh, I hate the poor. At least, I hate those dirty, drunken, disreputable people who live like pigs. If they must be provided for, let other people look after them. How can you expect any one to think well of us when such things are written about us in that infamous book?

SARTORIUS (*coldly and a little wistfully*). I see I have made a real lady of you, Blanche.

BLANCHE (*defiantly*). Well, are you sorry for that?

SARTORIUS. No, my dear, of course not. But do you know, Blanche, that my mother was a very poor woman, and that her poverty was not her fault?

BLANCHE. I suppose not; but the people we want to mix with now don't know that. And it was not my fault; so I don't see why *I* should be made to suffer for it.

SARTORIUS (*enraged*). Who makes you suffer for it, miss? What would you be now but for what your grandmother did for me when she stood at her wash-tub for thirteen hours a day and thought herself rich when she made fifteen shillings a week?

BLANCHE (*angrily*). I suppose I should have been down on her level instead of being raised above it, as I am now. Would you like us to go and live in that place in the book for the sake of grandmamma? I hate the idea of such things. I don't want to know about them. I love you because you brought me up to something better. (*Half aside, as she turns away from him.*) I should hate you if you had not.

SARTORIUS (*giving in*). Well, my child, I suppose it is natural for you to feel that way, after your bringing up. It is the ladylike view of the matter. So don't let us quarrel, my girl. You shall not be made to suffer any more. I have made up my mind to improve the property, and get in quite a new class of tenants. There! does that satisfy you? I am only waiting for the consent of the ground landlord, Lady Roxdale.

BLANCHE. Lady Roxdale!

SARTORIUS. Yes. But I shall expect the mortgagee to take his share of the risk.

BLANCHE. The mortgagee! Do you mean—— (*She cannot finish the sentence: Sartorius does it for her.*)

SARTORIUS. Harry Trench. Yes. And remember, Blanche : if he consents to join me in the scheme, I shall have to be friends with him.

BLANCHE. And to ask him to the house ?

SARTORIUS. Only on business. You need not meet him unless you like.

BLANCHE (*overwhelmed*). When is he coming ?

SARTORIUS. There is no time to be lost. Lickcheese has gone to ask him to come round.

BLANCHE (*in dismay*). Then he will be here in a few minutes! What shall I do ?

SARTORIUS. I advise you to receive him as if nothing had happened, and then go out and leave us to our business. You are not afraid to meet him ?

BLANCHE. Afraid! No, most certainly not. But—— (*Lickcheese's voice is heard without*). Here they are. Don't say I'm here, papa. (*She rushes away into the study. Lickcheese comes in with Trench and Cokane. Cokane shakes hands effusively with Sartorius. Trench, who is coarsened and sullen, and has evidently not been making the best of his disappointment, bows shortly and resentfully. Lickcheese covers the embarrassment of the position by talking cheerfully until they are all seated round the large table, Trench on the right, Cokane on the left; the other two between them, with Lickcheese next to Cokane.*)

LICKCHEESE. Here we are, all friends round St. Paul's. You remember Mr. Cokane: he does a little business for me now as a friend, and gives me a help with my correspondence—sekketary we call it. I've no litery style, and that's the truth; so Mr. Cokane kindly puts it into my letters and draft prospectuses and advertisements and the like. Don't you, Cokane ? Of course you do : why shouldn't you ? He's been helping me to-night to persuade his old friend, Dr. Trench, about the matter we were speaking of.

COKANE (*austerely*). No, Mr. Lickcheese, not trying to persuade him. No : this is a matter of principle with me. I say it is your duty, Henry — your d u t y — to put those abominable buildings into proper and habitable repair. As a man of science you owe it to the community to perfect the sanitary arrangements. In questions of duty there is no room for persuasion, even from the oldest friend.

SARTORIUS (*to Trench*). I certainly feel, as Mr. Cokane puts it, that it is our duty : one which I have perhaps too long neglected out of regard for the poorest class of tenants.

LICKCHEESE. Not a doubt of it, gents, a dooty. I can be as sharp as any man when it's a question of business ; but dooty's another thing.

TRENCH. Well, I don't see that it is any more my duty now than it was four months ago. I look at it simply as a question of so much money.

COKANE. Shame, Harry, shame ! Shame !

TRENCH. Oh, shut up, you fool. (*Cokane springs up. Lickcheese catches his coat and holds him.*)

LICKCHEESE. Steady, steady, Mr. Sekketary. Dr. Trench is only joking.

COKANE. I insist on the withdrawal of that expression. I have been called a fool.

TRENCH (*morosely*). So you are a fool.

COKANE. Then you are a damned fool. Now, sir !

TRENCH. All right. Now we've settled that. (*Cokane, with a snort, sits down.*) What I mean is this. Don't let's have any nonsense about this job. As I understand it, Robbins's Row is to be pulled down to make way for the new street into the Strand ; and the straight tip now is to go for compensation.

LICKCHEESE. (*chuckling*). That's so, Dr. Trench. That's it.

TRENCH (*continuing*). Well, it appears that the dirtier a place is, the more rent you get; and the decenter it is, the more compensation you get. So we're to give up dirt and go in for decency.

SARTORIUS. I should not put it exactly in that way; but——

COKANE. Quite right, Mr. Sartorius, quite right. The case could not have been stated with worse taste or with less tact.

LICKCHEESE. Sh-sh-sh-sh!

SARTORIUS. I do not quite go with you there, Mr. Cokane. Dr. Trench puts the case frankly as a man of business. I take the wider view of a public man. We live in a progressive age; and humanitarian ideas are advancing and must be taken into account. But my practical conclusion is the same as his. I should hardly feel justified in mak-a large claim for compensation under existing circumstances.

LICKCHEESE. Of course not: and you wouldn't get it if you did. You see, it's like this, Dr. Trench. There's no doubt that the Vestries has legal powers to play old Harry with slum properties, and spoil the housenacking game if they please. That didn't matter in the good old times, because the Vestries used to be ourselves. Nobody ever knew a word about the election; and we used to get ten of us into a room and elect one another, and do what we liked. Well, that cock won't fight any longer; and, to put it short, the game is up for men in the position of you and Mr. Sartorius. My advice to you is, take the present chance of getting out of it. Spend a little money on the block at the Cribbs Market end—enough to make it look like a model dwelling; and let the other block to me on fair terms for a depot of the North Thames Iced Mutton Company. They'll be knocked down inside of two year to make room for the new north and south main thoroughfare; and you'll be compensated to the tune of double the present valuation, with the cost of the improvements thrown in. Leave things as they are ; and you stand a good chance of being fined, or condemned, or pulled down before long. Now's your time.

COKANE. Hear, hear ! Hear, hear ! Hear, hear ! Admirably put from the business point of view ! I recognize the uselessness of putting the moral point of view to you, Trench ; but even you must feel the cogency of Mr. Lickcheese's business statement.

TRENCH. But why can't you act without me ? What have I got to do with it ? I am only a mortgagee.

SARTORIUS. There is a certain risk in this compensation investment, Dr. Trench. The County Council may alter the line of the new street. If that happens, the money spent in improving the houses will be thrown away—simply thrown away. Worse than thrown away, in fact ; for the new buildings may stand unlet or half let for years. But you will expect your seven per cent as usual.

TRENCH. A man must live.

COKANE. Je n'en vois pas la nécessité.

TRENCH. Shut up, Billy ; or else speak some language you understand. No, Mr. Sartorius : I should be very glad to stand in with you if I could afford it ; but I can't ; so there's an end of that.

LICKCHEESE. Well, all I can say is that you're a very foolish young man.

COKANE. What did I tell you, Harry ?

TRENCH. I don't see that it's any business of yours, Mr. Lickcheese.

LICKCHEESE. It's a free country: every man has a right to his opinion. (*Cokane cries* Hear, hear!) Come, where's your feelings for them poor people, Dr. Trench? Remember how it went to your heart when I first told you about them. What! are you going to turn hard?

TRENCH. No: it won't do: you can't get over me that way.

CPSIA information can be obtained
at www.ICGtesting.com
Printed in the USA
BVHW051040210721
612411BV00012B/3755